RAY

VOLATILE!

THE NATIONS
THE BIBLE SAYS WILL
ATTACK ISRAEL
IN THE LATTER DAYS

BRIDGE
LOGOS

Newberry, FL 32669

Volatile! The Nations the Bible Says Will Attack Israel in the Latter Days

Bridge-Logos, Inc.
Newberry, FL 32669, USA

Edited by Lynn Copeland

Page design and production by Genesis Group

ISBN 978-1-61036-988-6

Library of Congress Control Number: 2023950293

Printed in the United States of America

CONTENTS

PREFACE

In 1991, I wrote a book called *Russia Will Attack Israel*. In December of the same year, the Soviet Union collapsed. Suddenly Russia was no longer a superpower, then the Russian bear went into a long hibernation. So there goes that prophecy. But years later, it began to stir from its sleep, slowly stood to its feet, and was evidently very hungry.

When it attempted to devour Ukraine in February 2022, I remembered my book. I also remembered that whenever I shared my thoughts on Bible prophecy, it caused contention. This is because almost everyone has an opinion about eschatology (the end times). Some believe that what we see happening today in the Middle East has nothing to do with Scripture. They say that almost every prophecy was fulfilled before 70 AD when Jerusalem was ransacked by the Romans. Others believe in a partial fulfillment, and still others say that the prophesied events will happen in the future.

But when catastrophic events unfolded in Israel on October 7, 2023, a number of respected preachers came out of the closet and began talking about Russia and its place in prophecy. That emboldened me to publish this book. My sincere hope is that it helps you to realize that our timeless God knows the beginning from the end. And that should give us a great comfort in these dark and turbulent times.

INTRODUCTION

For your convenience, below are eight relevant prophetic passages of Scripture to which this book will often refer.

Ezekiel 38:1–23:

> [1] Now the word of the LORD came to me, saying, [2] "Son of man, set your face against Gog, of the land of Magog, the prince of Rosh, Meshech, and Tubal, and prophesy against him, [3] and say, 'Thus says the Lord GOD: "Behold, I am against you, O Gog, the prince of Rosh, Meshech, and Tubal. [4] I will turn you around, put hooks into your jaws, and lead you out, with all your army, horses, and horsemen, all splendidly clothed, a great company with bucklers and shields, all of them handling swords. [5] Persia, Ethiopia, and Libya are with them, all of them with shield and helmet; [6] Gomer and all its troops; the house of Togarmah from the far north and all its troops— many people are with you.
>
> [7] "Prepare yourself and be ready, you and all your companies that are gathered about you; and be a guard for them. [8] After many

days you will be visited. In the latter years you will come into the land of those brought back from the sword and gathered from many people on the mountains of Israel, which had long been desolate; they were brought out of the nations, and now all of them dwell safely. [9] You will ascend, coming like a storm, covering the land like a cloud, you and all your troops and many peoples with you."

[10] 'Thus says the Lord GOD: "On that day it shall come to pass that thoughts will arise in your mind, and you will make an evil plan: [11] You will say, 'I will go up against a land of unwalled villages; I will go to a peaceful people, who dwell safely, all of them dwelling without walls, and having neither bars nor gates'— [12] to take plunder and to take booty, to stretch out your hand against the waste places that are again inhabited, and against a people gathered from the nations, who have acquired livestock and goods, who dwell in the midst of the land. [13] Sheba, Dedan, the merchants of Tarshish, and all their young lions will say to you, 'Have you come to take plunder? Have you gathered your army to take booty, to carry away silver and gold, to take away livestock and goods, to take great plunder?' "'

[14] "Therefore, son of man, prophesy and say to Gog, 'Thus says the Lord GOD: "On that day when My people Israel dwell safely, will you not know it? [15] Then you will come from

your place out of the far north, you and many peoples with you, all of them riding on horses, a great company and a mighty army. ¹⁶ You will come up against My people Israel like a cloud, to cover the land. It will be in the latter days that I will bring you against My land, so that the nations may know Me, when I am hallowed in you, O Gog, before their eyes." ¹⁷ Thus says the Lord GOD: "Are you he of whom I have spoken in former days by My servants the prophets of Israel, who prophesied for years in those days that I would bring you against them?

¹⁸ "And it will come to pass at the same time, when Gog comes against the land of Israel," says the Lord GOD, "that My fury will show in My face. ¹⁹ For in My jealousy and in the fire of My wrath I have spoken: 'Surely in that day there shall be a great earthquake in the land of Israel, ²⁰ so that the fish of the sea, the birds of the heavens, the beasts of the field, all creeping things that creep on the earth, and all men who are on the face of the earth shall shake at My presence. The mountains shall be thrown down, the steep places shall fall, and every wall shall fall to the ground.' ²¹ I will call for a sword against Gog throughout all My mountains," says the Lord GOD. "Every man's sword will be against his brother. ²² And I will bring him to judgment with pestilence and bloodshed; I will rain down on him, on his

troops, and on the many peoples who are with him, flooding rain, great hailstones, fire, and brimstone. [23] Thus I will magnify Myself and sanctify Myself, and I will be known in the eyes of many nations. Then they shall know that I am the LORD." '

Ezekiel 39:1–16:

[1] "And you, son of man, prophesy against Gog, and say, 'Thus says the Lord GOD: "Behold, I am against you, O Gog, the prince of Rosh, Meshech, and Tubal; [2] and I will turn you around and lead you on, bringing you up from the far north, and bring you against the mountains of Israel. [3] Then I will knock the bow out of your left hand, and cause the arrows to fall out of your right hand. [4] You shall fall upon the mountains of Israel, you and all your troops and the peoples who are with you; I will give you to birds of prey of every sort and to the beasts of the field to be devoured. [5] You shall fall on the open field; for I have spoken," says the Lord GOD. [6] "And I will send fire on Magog and on those who live in security in the coastlands. Then they shall know that I am the LORD. [7] So I will make My holy name known in the midst of My people Israel, and I will not let them profane My holy name anymore. Then the nations shall know that I am the LORD, the Holy One in Israel. [8] Surely it is

coming, and it shall be done," says the Lord GOD. "This is the day of which I have spoken.

⁹ "Then those who dwell in the cities of Israel will go out and set on fire and burn the weapons, both the shields and bucklers, the bows and arrows, the javelins and spears; and they will make fires with them for seven years. ¹⁰ They will not take wood from the field nor cut down any from the forests, because they will make fires with the weapons; and they will plunder those who plundered them, and pillage those who pillaged them," says the Lord GOD.

¹¹ "It will come to pass in that day that I will give Gog a burial place there in Israel, the valley of those who pass by east of the sea; and it will obstruct travelers, because there they will bury Gog and all his multitude. Therefore they will call it the Valley of Hamon Gog. ¹²For seven months the house of Israel will be burying them, in order to cleanse the land. ¹³ Indeed all the people of the land will be burying, and they will gain renown for it on the day that I am glorified," says the Lord GOD. ¹⁴ "They will set apart men regularly employed, with the help of a search party, to pass through the land and bury those bodies remaining on the ground, in order to cleanse it. At the end of seven months they will make a search. ¹⁵ The search party will pass through the land; and when anyone sees a man's bone,

he shall set up a marker by it, till the buriers have buried it in the Valley of Hamon Gog. [16] The name of the city will also be Hamonah. Thus they shall cleanse the land."'

Joel 3:1,2:

[1] "For behold, in those days and at that time, When I bring back the captives of Judah and Jerusalem,

[2] I will also gather all nations, and bring them down to the Valley of Jehoshaphat; and I will enter into judgment with them there on account of My people, My heritage Israel, whom they have scattered among the nations; they have also divided up My land."

Zechariah 12:1–3,9:

[1] The burden of the word of the LORD against Israel. Thus says the LORD, who stretches out the heavens, lays the foundation of the earth, and forms the spirit of man within him: [2] "Behold, I will make Jerusalem a cup of drunkenness to all the surrounding peoples, when they lay siege against Judah and Jerusalem. [3] And it shall happen in that day that I will make Jerusalem a very heavy stone for all peoples; all who would heave it away will surely be cut in pieces, though all nations of the earth are gathered against it.

⁹ It shall be in that day that I will seek to destroy all the nations that come against Jerusalem.

Matthew 24:1–44:

¹ Then Jesus went out and departed from the temple, and His disciples came up to show Him the buildings of the temple. ² And Jesus said to them, "Do you not see all these things? Assuredly, I say to you, not one stone shall be left here upon another, that shall not be thrown down."

³ Now as He sat on the Mount of Olives, the disciples came to Him privately, saying, "Tell us, when will these things be? And what will be the sign of Your coming, and of the end of the age?"

⁴ And Jesus answered and said to them: "Take heed that no one deceives you. ⁵ For many will come in My name, saying, 'I am the Christ,' and will deceive many. ⁶ And you will hear of wars and rumors of wars. See that you are not troubled; for all these things must come to pass, but the end is not yet. ⁷ For nation will rise against nation, and kingdom against kingdom. And there will be famines, pestilences, and earthquakes in various places. ⁸ All these are the beginning of sorrows.

⁹ "Then they will deliver you up to tribulation and kill you, and you will be hated by all

VOLATILE!

nations for My name's sake. ¹⁰ And then many will be offended, will betray one another, and will hate one another. ¹¹ Then many false prophets will rise up and deceive many. ¹² And because lawlessness will abound, the love of many will grow cold.¹³ But he who endures to the end shall be saved. ¹⁴ And this gospel of the kingdom will be preached in all the world as a witness to all the nations, and then the end will come.

¹⁵ "Therefore when you see the 'abomination of desolation,' spoken of by Daniel the prophet, standing in the holy place" (whoever reads, let him understand), ¹⁶ "then let those who are in Judea flee to the mountains. ¹⁷ Let him who is on the housetop not go down to take anything out of his house. ¹⁸ And let him who is in the field not go back to get his clothes. ¹⁹ But woe to those who are pregnant and to those who are nursing babies in those days! ²⁰ And pray that your flight may not be in winter or on the Sabbath. ²¹ For then there will be great tribulation, such as has not been since the beginning of the world until this time, no, nor ever shall be. ²² And unless those days were shortened, no flesh would be saved; but for the elect's sake those days will be shortened.

²³ "Then if anyone says to you, 'Look, here is the Christ!' or 'There!' do not believe it. ²⁴ For false christs and false prophets will rise and show great signs and wonders to deceive, if

possible, even the elect. [25] See, I have told you beforehand.

[26] "Therefore if they say to you, 'Look, He is in the desert!' do not go out; or 'Look, He is in the inner rooms!' do not believe it. [27] For as the lightning comes from the east and flashes to the west, so also will the coming of the Son of Man be. [28] For wherever the carcass is, there the eagles will be gathered together.

[29] "Immediately after the tribulation of those days the sun will be darkened, and the moon will not give its light; the stars will fall from heaven, and the powers of the heavens will be shaken. [30] Then the sign of the Son of Man will appear in heaven, and then all the tribes of the earth will mourn, and they will see the Son of Man coming on the clouds of heaven with power and great glory. [31] And He will send His angels with a great sound of a trumpet, and they will gather together His elect from the four winds, from one end of heaven to the other.

[32] "Now learn this parable from the fig tree: When its branch has already become tender and puts forth leaves, you know that summer is near. [33] So you also, when you see all these things, know that it is near—at the doors! [34] Assuredly, I say to you, this generation will by no means pass away till all these things take place. [35] Heaven and earth will pass

away, but My words will by no means pass away.

[36] "But of that day and hour no one knows, not even the angels of heaven, but My Father only. [37] But as the days of Noah were, so also will the coming of the Son of Man be. [38] For as in the days before the flood, they were eating and drinking, marrying and giving in marriage, until the day that Noah entered the ark, [39] and did not know until the flood came and took them all away, so also will the coming of the Son of Man be. [40] Then two men will be in the field: one will be taken and the other left. [41] Two women will be grinding at the mill: one will be taken and the other left. [42] Watch therefore, for you do not know what hour your Lord is coming. [43] But know this, that if the master of the house had known what hour the thief would come, he would have watched and not allowed his house to be broken into.[44] Therefore you also be ready, for the Son of Man is coming at an hour you do not expect.

Luke 21:5–36:

[5] Then, as some spoke of the temple, how it was adorned with beautiful stones and donations, He said, [6] "These things which you see— the days will come in which not one stone shall be left upon another that shall not be thrown down."

[7] So they asked Him, saying, "Teacher, but when will these things be? And what sign will there be when these things are about to take place?"

[8] And He said: "Take heed that you not be deceived. For many will come in My name, saying, 'I am He,' and, 'The time has drawn near.' Therefore do not go after them. [9] But when you hear of wars and commotions, do not be terrified; for these things must come to pass first, but the end will not come immediately."

[10] Then He said to them, "Nation will rise against nation, and kingdom against kingdom. [11] And there will be great earthquakes in various places, and famines and pestilences; and there will be fearful sights and great signs from heaven. [12] But before all these things, they will lay their hands on you and persecute you, delivering you up to the synagogues and prisons. You will be brought before kings and rulers for My name's sake. [13] But it will turn out for you as an occasion for testimony. [14] Therefore settle it in your hearts not to meditate beforehand on what you will answer; [15] for I will give you a mouth and wisdom which all your adversaries will not be able to contradict or resist. [16] You will be betrayed even by parents and brothers, relatives and friends; and they will put some of you to death. [17] And you will be hated by all for My name's sake. [18] But

not a hair of your head shall be lost. [19] By your patience possess your souls.

[20] "But when you see Jerusalem surrounded by armies, then know that its desolation is near. [21] Then let those who are in Judea flee to the mountains, let those who are in the midst of her depart, and let not those who are in the country enter her. [22] For these are the days of vengeance, that all things which are written may be fulfilled. [23] But woe to those who are pregnant and to those who are nursing babies in those days! For there will be great distress in the land and wrath upon this people. [24] And they will fall by the edge of the sword, and be led away captive into all nations. And Jerusalem will be trampled by Gentiles until the times of the Gentiles are fulfilled.

[25] "And there will be signs in the sun, in the moon, and in the stars; and on the earth distress of nations, with perplexity, the sea and the waves roaring; [26] men's hearts failing them from fear and the expectation of those things which are coming on the earth, for the powers of the heavens will be shaken. [27] Then they will see the Son of Man coming in a cloud with power and great glory. [28] Now when these things begin to happen, look up and lift up your heads, because your redemption draws near."

[29] Then He spoke to them a parable: "Look at the fig tree, and all the trees. [30] When they

are already budding, you see and know for yourselves that summer is now near. [31] So you also, when you see these things happening, know that the kingdom of God is near. [32] Assuredly, I say to you, this generation will by no means pass away till all things take place. [33] Heaven and earth will pass away, but My words will by no means pass away.

[34] "But take heed to yourselves, lest your hearts be weighed down with carousing, drunkenness, and cares of this life, and that Day come on you unexpectedly. [35] For it will come as a snare on all those who dwell on the face of the whole earth. [36] Watch therefore, and pray always that you may be counted worthy to escape all these things that will come to pass, and to stand before the Son of Man."

1 Timothy 4:1–3:

[1] Now the Spirit expressly says that in latter times some will depart from the faith, giving heed to deceiving spirits and doctrines of demons, [2] speaking lies in hypocrisy, having their own conscience seared with a hot iron, [3] forbidding to marry, and commanding to abstain from foods which God created to be received with thanksgiving by those who believe and know the truth.

2 Timothy 3:1–5:

> [1] But know this, that in the last days perilous times will come: [2] For men will be lovers of themselves, lovers of money, boasters, proud, blasphemers, disobedient to parents, unthankful, unholy, [3] unloving, unforgiving, slanderers, without self-control, brutal, despisers of good, [4] traitors, headstrong, haughty, lovers of pleasure rather than lovers of God, [5] having a form of godliness but denying its power.

CHAPTER ONE

THE CONTENTIOUS ISSUE OF ROSH

After the horrifying events of October 7, 2023, when Hamas invaded Israel, brutally slaughtered over 1,400 innocent people, including babies, raped women and girls, and took 240 hostages, the fuse of the Middle East suddenly moved even closer to the dynamite. As Israel retaliated to defend herself, Muslim nations began to threaten Israel with war, with Russia also rattling its saber.

Around that time, I produced a video on the subject of Bible prophecy, "War in Israel is a Sign of the End of the Age," that quickly received over a million views. Of course, that opened the door to criticism from those who interpret prophecy differently. As a summary, here are the main beliefs about eschatology:

- Those who embrace *preterism* believe that many of the prophecies in the Bible, particularly those in the New Testament, were fulfilled in the past with the destruction of Jerusalem in 70 AD.

- Those who settle on *historicism* are convinced that biblical prophecies have been unfolding gradually throughout history, from the time they were written to the present and into the future.

- And those who believe in *futurism* take the stance that many biblical prophecies, particularly those in the books of Daniel and Revelation, are yet to be fulfilled in the future.

Here are some comments from our YouTube channel that show the differing eschatological views, particularly about the possibility that the word "Rosh," used in Scripture (such as Ezekiel 38:2: "Gog, of the land of Magog, the prince of Rosh, Meshech, and Tubal"), is a reference to Russia:

You abuse the words of Ezekiel. Today's Israel is a secular state and not God's nation. The

Jews have to accept Jesus as their Messiah. Rosh mean simply head or leader, not Russia.

This view was never taught or believed for 1,800 years. Those Old Testament prophecies have all been fulfilled, just as the first century disciples and apostles taught.

Rosh is not Russia. Russ came from Scandinavia…This eschatology is false.

The correct meaning of the common Hebrew word "Rosh" is "chief" or "head" and it does not in any way suggest Russia. The Zionist-steered Dispensationalists conveniently declare the obvious meaning of the word as incorrect so that their masters may fulfill a false prophecy these minions have concocted in reference to Russia.

One argument is that, despite Russia arming Islamic nations that hate Israel, this isn't a fulfillment of Ezekiel 38—because the word "Rosh" simply means "head" or "chief." But others disagree:

There is controversy over how the Hebrew word *rosh* should be translated in this verse. The King James Version uses the adjective "chief." But the correct rendering (used by the Moffatt, New King James and others) uses the word not as an adjective, but as a proper noun: Rosh. Thus, that verse should read, "the prince of Rosh, Meshech and Tubal." *Rosh* was the ancient name of Russia, once called *Rus*. Many encyclopedias and commentaries (such as the *Jamieson, Fausset and Brown Commentary*) recognize this.[1]

The discovery of Russia in Ezekiel's prophecy is not a fundamentalist invention of this mid-century...Long before Russia became the threat to world freedom, progress and peace she is today, Biblical scholars recognized her portrayal in Ezekiel.[2]

Gesenius says, "Without much doubt *Rosh* designates *the Russians*, who are described by the Byzantine writers of the 10th century, under the name of *the Roos*..."[3]

Magog is a land "in the far north," from Israel's point of view (Ezekiel 38:15; 39:2). Most Bible commentators interpret "Magog" as Russia—and, indeed, Russia is straight north of Israel, all the way up to the Arctic Circle. According

to this view, "Rosh" is a reference to Russia, "Meshek" is either Moscow or the people north of the Black Sea (the area of southern Russia and Ukraine), and "Tubal," which is always listed with Meshek in Scripture, is identified as a city in Siberia or an area in central Turkey.[4]

The Islamic connection of the Ezekiel 38 invasion force is inescapable. It is this connection and Russia's desire to resume "super power" status in the region that may be the "hook" that draws Russia into the conflict.[5]

Why would Russia have any interest in supporting Muslim nations in their fight against Israel?

According to Mufti Ravil Gaynutdin, chairman of the Religious Board of Muslims of the Russian Federation, there were 25 million Muslims in 2018, approximately 18 percent of the population.[6]

Military cooperation between Iran and Russia has gyrated from virtually nothing after the 1979 revolution to a strategic partnership, bolstered by important arms transfers, by 2023. Overall, Moscow accounted for about a third of Tehran's arms imports during the four decades after the revolution, according to data from the Stockholm International Peace Research Institute (SIPRI). And the Islamic Republic was exporting Iranian arms to Russia for its invasion of Ukraine. The two countries had forged a "full-scale defense partnership" by mid-2023, according to John Kirby of the National Security Council.[7]

The following is a transcript of a very moving conversation I had with a Jewish mathematics professor at a college in California. Most people don't realize that Christianity has its roots in Judaism. Jesus was Jewish. So were His disciples. So were the first eight thousand Christians. Christianity began in Jerusalem, and the Scriptures say it went to the Jew first (see Romans 1:16). And yet most of us cringe at the thought of sharing Jesus with a Jewish person. This need not be, as you will see with this amazing conversation.

RAY: You're a math teacher at this college that I've been coming to almost every day for about fourteen years, and you spoke about your colleague who is on staff—a very intelligent gentleman, who spoke very quickly—and he's a delightful character. And you watched that interview on YouTube, is that correct?[8]

RUBEN: Yes.

RAY: And what did you get out of it?

RUBEN: What I got out of it was that Micky doesn't believe. He doesn't believe in God. He believes that maybe some Master Creator created everything, but he doesn't believe in a human "corporeal," I think that's what you say, God, living God.

RAY: So, are you Jewish?

RUBEN: Yes.

RAY: Are you a Christian?

RUBEN: No.

RAY: Now, you said something to me about being troubled. What did you mean?

RUBEN: Well, I saw your video with Micky, and I'm concerned, and I'm going be real honest, I'm concerned about my immortal soul. As a Jew I'm very uncomfortable talking about it because we're told to be very careful. The Christian faith is based on Judaism; it's out of context—that the Messiah will not be man, of man.

RAY: Ruben, I'm Jewish. Did you know that?

RUBEN: No, I didn't know that.

RAY: My mother's full Jew.

RUBEN: Oh my goodness, that's wild.

RAY: So, you can be very relaxed, because this is just a couple of Jews chatting…

RUBEN: That's wild.

RAY: If you ever read the Scriptures, the Old Testament, they speak of the Jewish Messiah. Isaiah 53 can't be the nation of Israel. It speaks of a man, says He was "a man of sorrows, and acquainted with grief," speaking of the Messiah. So, how're you doing with the Law of Moses? We went through the Law with your colleague, our intelligent friend.

RUBEN: Not so good. I've also watched other of your videos and I'm a lying, cheating, blasphemous …I can't remember the last—

RAY: Adulterer at heart.

RUBEN: Adulterer at heart. Yes.

RAY: So, where are you going when you die?

RUBEN: We don't—as Jews, we don't spend a lot of time thinking about that. We spend our time thinking about making heaven on earth.

RAY: It's not working, is it?

RUBEN: Not at all.

RAY: It's a real mess! Yes, the Bible's the instruction book, and humanity's thrown away the instruction book. Have you ever tried putting together an appliance and not looked at the instructions first, and it's a mess, and then you go to the instructions after the thing's a mess? That's what humanity has done with God's Word. Do you understand the gospel?

RUBEN: The Christian gospel?

RAY: Well, the gospel is the good news that God sent a Messiah to suffer and die on the cross. Let's go back to Moses where they slew an animal, a lamb, that would be a covering for sin temporarily. Like the Passover. You celebrate Passover?

RUBEN: Not so often.

RAY: Do you understand what it means? That you put the blood of the lamb on the doorposts and death passed over—

RUBEN: The children.

RAY: —the children [of Israel], because they had the faith to trust in God to put that blood on the door. It's a crazy thing to do, but they did it and death passed over. When John the Baptist, who was a Jew, saw Jesus the first time, who was a Jew, he said, "Behold the Lamb of God, who takes away the sin of the world!" God provided a lamb. Do you remember the story of Isaac and Abraham? Abraham was going to slay Isaac and God gave him a ram that was caught in the thicket. And Abraham said, "God Himself will provide a lamb." And that's what God did through Jesus. The Bible says He was the Lamb of God, slain from the foundation of the world. So, when Jesus came to this earth, the Bible says He was God in human form. Isaiah 9, Old Testament: "Unto us a Child is born, unto us a Son is given,…and His name shall be called Wonderful." That's what the Bible says. God gave a Son. Psalm 2 says, "Kiss the

Son, lest He be angry, and you perish in the way, when His wrath is kindled but a little." Jesus called Himself the Son of God, but the Bible actually tells us He was God in human form, the express image of the invisible God, because the Lamb of God had to be perfect, without sin. And so, when God created for Himself a body and filled that body as a hand fills a glove, we're looking at God manifest in the flesh.

RUBEN: Wow!

RAY: Wow is the word. It's just awe-inspiring. So, when Jesus suffered and died on the cross and cried out, "It is finished," He was saying the debt has been paid. God's Law is satisfied. Like in a court of law, when someone pays your fine the judge says, "You're out of here. Someone's paid your fine. The law is satisfied." But when Jesus cried out, "It is finished," He was saying the Law of God is satisfied. And that means God can legally grant us everlasting life. He can dismiss our case, let us live forever, legally, all because of the fact that Jesus suffered and died on the cross to take the punishment for the sin of the world.

RUBEN: Wow.

RAY: And then He rose from the dead and defeated death. And if you'll repent of your sins and trust in Jesus, the Bible says God will remit your sins in a second and grant you everlasting life as a free gift;

not because *you're* good, but because *He's* good and kind and rich in mercy. So, are you sorry for your sins?

RUBEN: Yes.

RAY: Did you know that's called contrition? Did you know that?

RUBEN: No.

RAY: Yes, the Bible says, "Godly sorrow works repentance." And so, when you've got a contrite heart, that brings about genuine sorrow for sin, or repentance. The Bible speaks of "repentance unto life." So, are you ready to repent and put your faith in Jesus?

RUBEN: I don't know. I'm afraid.

RAY: What are you afraid of? God is the God of Israel and He's the lover of your soul. And you've said you were praying to meet me, weren't you?

RUBEN: Yes.

RAY: Hasn't God answered your prayer today?

RUBEN: Yes.

RAY: And so, just take a little step of faith and say, "God, I trust You with this. I'm going to yield my life to You and ask You to forgive my sins because of what Jesus did on the cross."

RUBEN: Is that all it takes?

RAY: It's so simple a child can understand it. Jesus said unless you become as a little child you cannot enter the Kingdom of God. Have you ever heard the story of the Prodigal Son?

RUBEN: I've heard of it. I couldn't quote it.

RAY: Let me share it with you. A young man went to his dad. And he says, "Dad, I want my inheritance now. That which is due to me." So, the dad gave him his inheritance. And he went to a far country. And the Bible says he wanted to spend it on riotous living and prostitutes. So he went to a far country, away from his father. And a famine came on the land, and he saw he was desiring pig food as he sat in a pigsty because that's the only job he could get. And he thought, "My father's servants have got it better than I. I'll go back to my father and say, 'I've sinned against heaven and in your sight. Take me on as your hired servant.'" So, he got up from that pigsty and went back to his father.

And the Bible says his father saw him from a great way off, and he ran to him. This is a Jewish father running to a rebellious son. He put his arms around him, fell upon his neck, and kissed him. And he said, "Bring a robe for my son. Bring a ring for his finger, and shoes for his feet, because my son was once dead but now he's alive!" And that's a picture of God's love for you. You've been a rebel, turned your back on God, and desired unclean things—pig food—and yet God runs to meet you halfway. That's what the Bible teaches. That's what Jesus was teaching. If I were you, I'd just say, "God, be merciful to me, a sinner; please forgive my sins."

RUBEN: Be merciful to me, please. Forgive my sins.

RAY: Let's bow in prayer, and I'll pray for you.

RUBEN: I don't know how.

RAY: I'll pray for you, okay? Father, I pray for Ruben. Thank You for this divine encounter today. I thank You for Your love for him and the fact that you've made provision for his forgiveness of sins. You've provided a Jewish Messiah to suffer for us, so that we could have a righteous standing in Your sight—not because of our goodness but because of Your kindness. I pray that You'll help Ruben today, give him peace of heart and peace of mind to know that he's made the right decision to put his trust in Jesus and to follow You. In Jesus' name we pray, amen.

RUBEN: Amen.

RAY: Do you have a Bible at home?

RUBEN: A Torah.

RAY: You have thirty minutes?

RUBEN: Yes.

RAY: I'll take you to our ministry and give you [a Bible and] some free stuff!

CHAPTER TWO

THE INTELLECTUAL PEG

Does the word "Rosh" refer to Russia? It certainly appears that way from Scripture as well as from unfolding current events. One thing I do know is that when I refer to Bible prophecy (as you will see from further encounters at the end of each chapter), it certainly catches the ears of unbelievers, and it then widens their eyes to the claims of the gospel.

Bible prophecy is a legitimate peg on which an unbeliever can hang his intellectual hat. It is evidence that God told us the end from the beginning. It gets the attention of a world that normally sees Christians as nothing but kooks and the Bible as childish fiction. If we steer away from prophecy in our witnessing because it's controversial, we are throwing aside an effective way to convince unbelievers to believe. The apostle Paul saw its value as he shared the gospel with unbelievers:

> So when they had appointed him a day, many came to him at his lodging, to whom he explained and solemnly testified of the king-

dom of God, persuading them concerning Jesus from both the Law of Moses *and the Prophets*, from morning till evening. (Acts 28:23, emphasis added)

How did Paul persuade unbelievers concerning Jesus? He did it from the Law of Moses *and* from the prophets. The Law of Moses addresses the conscience, and prophecy addresses the intellect. When we take someone through the Ten Commandments, the conscience echoes that they are right. That produces a knowledge of sin, guilt, and the need for mercy. Prophecy gives credibility to the Scriptures. The Bible's thousands of fulfilled prophecies provide powerful evidence that it is the Word of an all-knowing God and can be trusted.

We shouldn't therefore ignore this amazing bridge simply because Christians can't find a consensus. Most of us can't agree when it comes to who we should vote for; the issues of Calvinism and Arminianism; when, how, and by whom new believers should be baptized; how we should take communion—wine or grape juice, bread or crackers, etc. And human nature is such that when we make up our minds about these issues, we often hold onto our convictions with gritted teeth. This is because we are sure that we have it right—and that's never more evident than with interpretations of prophecy.

The following is a transcript from an interview I did with a very thoughtful and intelligent man at

Huntington Beach, California. My opening question to him was, "Have you been following the 2023 war in Israel?":

JACKSON: The Middle East is a really dangerous place. These are not good people. I don't know Palestine versus Hamas, I don't know…I know Hamas is evil. I've never seen anything like what I've seen. The videos you can see on social media are the most horrible things you ever, never want to see.

RAY: Do you ever study Bible prophecy?

JACKSON: No, no.

RAY: Did you know this is mentioned in the Scriptures again and again?

JACKSON: No.

RAY: God promised to scatter Israel throughout the whole world—the Jews—and then draw them back to Israel, and then promised they'd get Jerusalem. And that happened in 1967. In 1948 they became a state. Did you know in the Old Testament God promised He would destroy death, and the New Testament tells us how He did it? Did you know that?

JACKSON: No, no. How does He destroy death?

RAY: I'll share with you about how the Bible says God destroyed death, but to do so I have to give you some bad news. Like a doctor who wants to give a cure for cancer to someone, the patient must know he's got a terminal disease or he's not going to appreciate the cure. Does that make sense?

JACKSON: Yes.

RAY: So, I'm going to share the disease with you: do you think you're a good person?

JACKSON: I try to be.

RAY: How many lies have you told? That's the Ninth Commandment.

JACKSON: Many.

RAY: Ever stolen something in your whole life, even if it's small?

JACKSON: Yes, once.

RAY: So, you're a lying thief?

JACKSON: Yes.

RAY: Have you ever used God's name in vain?

JACKSON: Yeah, yeah.

RAY: Jackson, the Bible says we're in a state of hostility toward God, and there's no greater evidence of a hostile mind than that you take your Creator's name —the One who gave you life—His holy name, and use it in place of a cuss word. We don't do that with Hitler's name or Mussolini's or anyone's. Only Jesus Christ and God. And it shows our state of hostility. And the Bible even pinpoints why we're hostile. It says we don't want God telling us what to do morally.

JACKSON: Yes. I would agree with all of that. It's probably very much engrained in Western culture.

RAY: Certainly is. This one's the one that nailed me many years ago: Jesus said, "Whoever looks upon a woman to lust for her has committed adultery already with her in his heart." Have you ever looked at a woman with lust?

JACKSON: Yes.

RAY: Sex before marriage?

JACKSON: Yes.

RAY: So, here's a quick summation of your court case on Judgment Day. Jackson, you just told me you're a lying, thieving, blasphemous, fornicating, self-righteous adulterer at heart, and you have to face God on Judgment Day. If He judges you by the Ten Commandments, are you going to be innocent or guilty?

JACKSON: Oh...guilty!

RAY: Ever heard the Bible verse "the wages of sin is death"? It's very famous.

JACKSON: No.

RAY: It's saying that God is paying you in death for your sins. Like a judge looks at a heinous criminal who's committed multiple murders but insists he's a good person. The judge says, "I'm going to show you how serious your crime is. I'm giving you the death sentence. This is your wages, this is what we're paying you. This is what you've earned." And Jackson, sin is so serious to a holy God, He's given you the death sentence. You're on Death Row. Your death will be evidence to you that God is deadly serious about sin…and you've earned your wages. So, if you're guilty on Judgment Day, would you go to Heaven or Hell?

JACKSON: Hell.

RAY: And does that concern you?

JACKSON: Yes.

RAY: It horrifies me. I've just met you, but I love you and I don't want you to go to Hell! It breaks my heart. Now this brings us out of the disease into the cure. I'm going to share the gospel with you. And Jackson, if you can get a grip of this, it's going to change everything for you. The Ten Commandments are called the moral Law. You and I broke the Law, and Jesus paid the fine. That's why He said, "It is finished!" just before He died. He cried that out on the cross: "It is finished!" He was saying "paid in full." If you're in court and you've got speeding fines, a judge will let you go if someone pays those fines.

He'll say, "You're guilty, Jackson, but you're out of here. Someone paid your fine." And it's legal. They'll let you go. Well, God can legally take the death sentence off you all because of what Jesus on the cross, through His death and resurrection. And all you have to do to find everlasting life is to repent of your sins—old-fashioned word, means to turn from them—and trust in Jesus like you trust a parachute. Now, if you're going to jump out of a plane at 10,000 feet, why would you put on a parachute?

JACKSON: So you don't hit the ground really hard.

RAY: And your motivation is fear. And that fear is your friend. It's not your enemy, because it's making you put a parachute on. It's doing you a favor. And Jackson, because I love you, I've tried to put the fear of God in you today. I've tried to make you sweat a little, make your heart palpitate, make your mouth go dry, hoping you'll see that fear is your friend, not your enemy, because it'll make you mean business with God. It'll make you serious about the issue of eternity. It'll drive you to the foot of the cross where you'll find God's gift of everlasting life. Is this making sense?

JACKSON: Yes, yes.

RAY: Are you going to think about what we've talked about?

JACKSON: Yes.

RAY: When are you going to repent and put your faith in Jesus?

JACKSON: That's a good question. I have a lot more questions. I don't know.

RAY: What are your other questions?

JACKSON: The list of the other Ten Commandments—do they ever involve not killing, when to kill, when it's...

RAY: The Eighth Commandment speaks of murder. And that's different than killing. The Scriptures make provision for you to protect your family. If someone's going to stab your wife with a knife and the only way you can stop him is to shoot him, the Scriptures say that's okay.

JACKSON: What if the enemy's going to shoot your wife and they're hiding behind a child? You have no choice.

RAY: Yes, you've got to protect them. What other commandments are stopping you coming to Christ? It's not commandments that are stopping you coming to Christ. It's your love of sin. That's what the Bible says.

JACKSON: I agree with you on that.

RAY: Examine my tone. Why am I talking to you with such earnestness? It's because I know what I'm saying is true and I really do care about you!

JACKSON: I see that.

RAY: I really care about you, and I want you to come to Christ and not put it off, because Satan's real—the Bible calls him the god of this world, he blinds the minds of those who don't believe, tries to stop you from coming to Christ. And you've got to give up the battle and say, "God, I'm a sinner. Please forgive me. I need a new, clean heart, that loves You and serves You and thirsts for righteousness." And that's what'll happen if you become a Christian. Any of your friends Christians?

JACKSON: Yes, most of them, yes.

RAY: And they're all praying for you.

JACKSON: Yes.

RAY: So, this is an answer to their prayers, so what are you waiting for?

JACKSON: Okay.

RAY: When are you going to repent and put your faith in Jesus?

JACKSON: I need to read more of the Bible. I would.

RAY: Okay, let me give you a quick analogy. You and I are on the edge of a plane, 10,000 feet up. I've got my parachute on, you don't have yours on. We're both going to jump any second. And I say, "Jackson! When are you going to put your parachute on?" "I need to read more about parachutes." So, the best thing I can do for you is to hang you out of the plane by your ankles for five seconds, pull you back in, and you'll say, "Give me that parachute!" Because you've seen the issues. And you're on the edge of eternity. Man, you could die today. Heart give out, you could get shot, you could die in your sleep, get an aneurism, so this is deadly serious. Can you hear what I'm saying?

JACKSON: Yes, I'll take a parachute. What if I'm not sure yet which parachute I'd like to take?

RAY: Well, you don't have any choices. There's only one parachute given by God, that's what the Bible says. "Neither is there salvation in any other. There is no other name under heaven given among men whereby we must be saved." Hinduism doesn't offer a savior; Islam doesn't offer a savior.

JACKSON: I know, but Jesus was a Jew.

RAY: Let me give you a little history lesson. Jesus was a Jew; all the disciples were Jewish; He was the Jewish Messiah; the first eight thousand people to become Christians were Jewish. Christianity is Jewish; it finds its roots in Jerusalem and that's where it started. So, this is a Jewish religion that blossomed into something called Christianity.

JACKSON: Right.

RAY: I'm Jewish. This is the promised Messiah, and the Bible says, "Put on the Lord Jesus Christ." You have no choice. Either jump without a Savior into eternity and get justice or take God as your Savior and have everlasting life. Man, there's a battle for your soul going on, so please, please, think about this with a sense of sobriety. I know what you're going through. I've been through what you're going through, that battle. The Bible says we're like men groping in darkness. Blind men, you know? And God says, "Just call upon Me and I'll give you light." This is what Jesus said: "I am the light of the world. He who follows Me shall not walk in darkness, but have the light of life." So, God will give you light if you call upon Him. Can you see the battle that's going on in your mind?

JACKSON: Yes.

RAY: Can I pray with you?

JACKSON: Absolutely.

RAY: Let's bow in prayer. Father, I pray for Jackson. We've all been through what he's going through—a battle for his soul. We wrestle not against flesh and blood, but against demonic forces. I pray today You'll reach and touch him, pull him out of the darkness into the glorious light. Grant him repentance, grant him understanding. May he see the issues and think of the sobering words of Jesus, "What will it profit a man if he gains the whole world, and loses his own soul?" In Jesus' name we pray, amen.

JACKSON: Amen.

RAY: Can I give you a book that I've written called *Scientific Facts in the Bible*?

JACKSON: Yes.

RAY: And I'm going to give you a Gospel of John, which is the fourth book of the New Testament, and a little booklet called "Save Yourself Some Pain," which is principles of Christian growth.

JACKSON: What do you have to say about the different Bibles? You said the book of John? What's— I've never known the difference. That's one reason.

RAY: Well, there's Matthew, Mark, Luke, and John. They're four Gospels, four different perspectives, four witnesses of the life of Christ. They all harmonize and they're just all pointing to Jesus and what He did on the cross. So, this is just the fourth book of the New Testament. Regarding all the Bibles, there's lots of different versions and they haven't changed. We've got versions for the Russians, versions for the Chinese, versions for the Germans, American version, the old English version, but they all say the same thing: that God offers everlasting life to those who repent and trust in Christ. Let me get that book for you... Great to meet you, Jackson, and I'm so pleased you're going to think about what we talked about.

JACKSON: Absolutely.

CHAPTER THREE

MY ESCHATOLOGICAL PILE

The disagreements that come with prophetic inter-pretations aren't confined to the identity of Rosh. Luke 21, Matthew 24, and the books of Timothy give a list of signs of the end of the age, but these signs are hotly contested. The issue isn't their legitimacy. It's whether or not these have been fulfilled in the past, are being fulfilled at present, or will be fulfilled in the future. Here are the signs:

From Matthew 24:

- False messiahs and false prophets arising
- Wars and rumors of war
- Nation rising against nation and kingdom against kingdom
- Famines and earthquakes in various places
- Pestilences or plagues
- Persecution of believers

- Betrayal and hatred among people
- Many falling away from the faith
- False prophets rising up and deceiving many
- The love of many growing cold
- The gospel being preached to all nations
- The "abomination of desolation" spoken of by the prophet Daniel
- Great tribulation, unprecedented since the beginning of the world
- False messiahs and false prophets performing great signs and wonders to deceive

From Luke 21:

- Wars and commotions
- Nation rising against nation and kingdom against kingdom
- Great earthquakes in various places
- Famines and pestilences
- Fearful sights and great signs from heaven
- Persecution, hatred, and betrayal of believers
- Destruction of Jerusalem
- Jerusalem being trampled by Gentiles until the times of the Gentiles are fulfilled

From 1 Timothy 4:

- Departure from the faith

- Listening to deceiving spirits and doctrines of demons
- Speaking lies in hypocrisy
- Consciences seared with a hot iron
- Forbidding to marry and commanding to abstain from certain foods

From 2 Timothy 3:

- Perilous times in the last days
- People who are lovers of themselves, lovers of money, boastful, proud, blasphemers, disobedient to their parents, ungrateful, unholy
- Without love, unforgiving, slanderous, without self-control, brutal, despisers of what is good
- Traitors, headstrong, haughty, lovers of pleasure rather than lovers of God
- Having a form of godliness but denying its power
- Always learning but never able to come to a knowledge of the truth

LIKE PLAYING JENGA

You may have played Jenga, a simple but interesting game. You remove small wooden blocks (about the size of your forefinger) one at a time from a tower, and then gently place them on top of the pile. As the tower grows, the winner is the last person to take a turn before it collapses.

For many years, I have found that prophecy has been like playing Jenga. I would look at the signs of Matthew 24 and Luke 21 and note how they perfectly matched the present day. But when I tried to place one particular verse onto the pile, the entire pile came crashing down.

Here's my pile from Luke 21:24–33: Signs in the sun, distress of nations, perplexity, and men's hearts failing them for fear. These are all happening nowadays. But then I see verse 32:

> "Assuredly, I say to you, this generation will by no means pass away till all things take place."

Down comes my eschatological pile. Those signs must have been around before 70 AD. But this explanation brings up a further problem. In Matthew 24, when the disciples asked about the future, Jesus spoke of wars and rumors of wars, nation rising against nation and kingdom against kingdom, famines, pestilences, and earthquakes in various places, persecution, and lawlessness. Then in verse 14 He added,

> "This good news of the kingdom [the gospel] will be preached throughout the whole world as a testimony to all the nations, and then the end [of the age] will come." (Matthew 24:14, AMP)

By 70 AD the gospel hadn't been preached throughout the whole world to *all* the nations. To make the signs fit the 70 AD interpretation, one is forced to put in a word that isn't there and assert this was a reference only to the "known" world. In other words, when Jesus said "the whole world" and "all the nations," He didn't mean the *whole* world and *all* the nations. History shows us that the gospel didn't get to most of the world until hundreds of years later. After speaking of these signs, Jesus then pointed to His second coming:

> "For as the lightning comes from the east and flashes to the west, so also will the coming of the Son of Man be...And they will see the Son of Man coming on the clouds of heaven with power and great glory." (Matthew 24:27,30)

There is a rift among those who hold to the various eschatological views, and no one wants to give up any land. However, there is a biblical principle that has the miracle-working ability to bring peace between these factions. It is a strange but enlightening proposition that is often used in Scripture, and it immediately lifts the fog of confusion. An example of this is the promised coming of the Messiah:

> "For unto us a child *is* born..." [Isaiah 9:6, emphasis added]. This was some seven centuries before the actual birth of the Lord. Edward J. Young observed: "He speaks of the birth as though it has already occurred, even though from his standpoint it was yet to take

place in the future" (*The Book of Isaiah*, Grand Rapids: Eerdmans, 1965, Vol. I, p. 329).[9]

This uses a figure of speech where a writer symbolically represents what is expected to occur at a later time. God declared it, and it will surely happen. This is how these signs could have existed both before *and* after 70 AD. Consider this comprehensive explanation from GotQuestions.org:

A double fulfillment or dual fulfillment of a Bible prophecy is the circumstance in which the prophecy has both a short-term and long-term fulfillment. A prophecy is made, and the first fulfillment comes to pass relatively soon thereafter. Later, there is a second fulfillment to the prophecy, and that second fulfillment is usually fuller and more literal. So, there is a "near" fulfillment and a "far" fulfillment. A prophecy having a dual fulfillment helps to unify Scripture and emphasizes God's masterful control of events. There are several examples of prophecies with a double fulfillment. Here are a few:

Joel's Holy Spirit Prophecy
The prophet Joel, speaking of the day of the Lord, said, "And afterward, I will pour out my Spirit on all people. Your sons and daughters will prophesy, your old men will dream dreams, your young men will see visions. Even on my servants, both men and women, I will

pour out my Spirit in those days" (Joel 2:28–29). The first fulfillment of this prophecy is when Peter stood up on the day of Pentecost and spoke the same words to those gathered in Jerusalem (Acts 2:14–18). Indeed, miraculous manifestations of God's power through the Holy Spirit happened on that day (Acts 2:1–13). However, that was only a partial fulfillment of Joel's prophecy. The prophecy goes on to speak of "blood and fire and billows of smoke" (Joel 2:30), astronomical signs (verse 31), and the gathering of all nations for judgment (Joel 3:1–2). None of that has yet happened; therefore, the ultimate fulfillment of Joel 2 awaits Jesus' second coming. At that time, God's enemies will experience "the great and dreadful day of the Lord" (Joel 2:31; cf. Revelation 16:14–16).

Isaiah's Virgin Birth Prophecy
In Isaiah 7 the Aramites and Israelites were seeking to conquer Jerusalem, and King Ahaz of Judah was fearful. The prophet Isaiah approaches King Ahaz and declares that Aram and Israel would not be successful in their conquest (Isaiah 7:7–9). The Lord offers Ahaz the opportunity to receive a sign (verse 10), but Ahaz refuses to put God to the test (verse 11). God responds by giving the sign Ahaz should look for: "The virgin will be with child and will give birth to a son...but before the

boy knows enough to reject the wrong and choose the right, the land of the two kings you dread will be laid waste" (Isaiah 7:14). So, Isaiah referred to a woman—a virgin when the prophecy was made—who would become pregnant and bear a son; a few years after that, Israel and Aram would be destroyed. That was the "near" fulfillment. In the New Testament, the apostle Matthew connects the virgin birth of Jesus (Matthew 1:23) with the prophecy in Isaiah 7:14. Jesus' virgin birth is the "far" fulfillment—fuller and more complete. Isaiah 7:14 is therefore a "double-fulfillment prophecy." It refers to the situation King Ahaz was facing but also to the coming Messiah who would be the ultimate deliverer.

Samuel's Prophecy to David

The prophet Samuel had a prophecy for King David that details a promise directly from God concerning David's son: "The LORD declares to you that the LORD himself will establish a house for you; when your days are over and you rest with your ancestors, I will raise up your offspring to succeed you, your own flesh and blood, and I will establish his kingdom. He is the one who will build a house for my Name, and I will establish the throne of his kingdom forever" (2 Samuel 7:11–13). David's son Solomon would become king and ultimately build the temple, thus partially fulfilling this prophecy. The complete fulfillment, however, is found in Christ, the Son of David. At the annunciation, the angel Gabriel said about Jesus, "The Lord God will give him the throne of his father David, and he will reign over Jacob's descendants forever; his kingdom will never end" (Luke 1:32–33). Right now, Jesus is building His church, a "house" for God's name (Matthew 16:18). He will become the eternal king on David's throne and establish the Holy City, the new Jerusalem (Revelation 21:2). Solomon was the partial fulfillment of Samuel's words, but Jesus is "greater than Solomon" and the more thorough fulfillment (Matthew 12:42).

Jesus' Second Coming Prophecy
While Jesus was teaching His disciples about the end times, they asked Him, "When will these things happen? And what will be the sign that they are about to take place?" (Luke 21:7). Jesus answers with a long discourse, which includes this warning: "When you see Jerusalem being surrounded by armies, you will know that its desolation is near. Then let those who are in Judea flee to the mountains, let those in the city get out, and let those in the country not enter the city" (Luke 21:20–21). Some Bible scholars believe that this prophecy was completely fulfilled in AD 70 when the Romans leveled Jerusalem. However,

Jesus goes on to give additional details about this time. He says, "There will be signs in the sun, moon and stars. On the earth, nations will be in anguish and perplexity at the roaring and tossing of the sea. People will faint from terror, apprehensive of what is coming on the world, for the heavenly bodies will be shaken. At that time they will see the Son of Man coming in a cloud with power and great glory" (Luke 21:25–27). It is clear by these additional details that the ultimate fulfillment of this prophecy is yet to come.

Ezekiel's Gog and Magog Prophecy
Another prophecy with a dual fulfillment is Ezekiel's prophecy of the battle of Gog and Magog. This prophecy is different in that *both* fulfillments are yet future. Ezekiel 38–39 predicts that Gog of the land of Magog will lead a great army that attacks the land of Israel, which is "peaceful and unsuspecting" at the time (Ezekiel 38:11). Magog will not win, because God will intervene to preserve Israel (Ezekiel 38:19–22). Gog and Magog are mentioned again in Revelation 20:7–8 in reference to a different battle. In Revelation, history will repeat itself in a final, end-times attack on the nation of Israel (Revelation 20:8–9). The result of this battle is that all Israel's enemies are destroyed, and Satan finds his place in the lake of fire (Revelation 20:10). Neither of

these two battles, both named Gog and Magog, has occurred yet.[10]

The following interview was recorded in Huntington Beach, California. Calvin was very open and respectful. Tyler was an atheist:

RAY: So, you believe in God?

CALVIN: Yes, sir.

RAY: Do you ever read the Bible?

CALVIN: Uh, no. No, I have not.

RAY: Do you ever study Bible prophecy?

CALVIN: I have looked at a few things, just in class and stuff like that, but never really sat down and committed that much to it.

TYLER: I wish there was a heavenly Father that created us all in His image and stuff and looks after us. But from all the stuff that I see—Covid and all the sex trafficking, and all this horrible stuff going on—this isn't good work that He's doing.

RAY: Well, this shows the sinful heart of mankind. That's all it shows.

TYLER: I didn't do nothing wrong.

RAY: Have you ever looked at a woman with lust?

TYLER: Don't we all?

RAY: Jesus said when you do that you commit adultery in your heart. Have you lied and stolen in your life?

TYLER: Sure.

RAY: So, you're a lying thief. You're in big trouble on Judgment Day.

TYLER: Boy, you sure come [laughing]...I wouldn't talk like that to you.

RAY: I know you wouldn't, because you're a professing atheist. Have you ever used God's name in vain?

TYLER: Probably, during anger.

RAY: Well, that's blasphemy, using God's holy name as a cuss word.

TYLER: Do you believe in the Bible?

RAY: Of course.

TYLER: Okay, do you kill your neighbor if you see him working on Sunday?

RAY: No.

TYLER: Why not? That's in the Bible!

RAY: The Bible doesn't say to do that. We're to love our enemies and do good to those who spitefully use us.

RAY [to Calvin]: Jesus said if you look at a woman and lust for her you commit adultery with her in your heart. When'd you last lust after a woman?

CALVIN: Nah... [laughing], that's...

RAY: That's the one that gets us. I mean, that's the one that got, Calvin. That made me realize I was a sinner, and I was in big trouble. Let's go through the other Commandments. Just stay with me for a minute. I know it's uncomfortable but it's worth it. How many lies have you told in your life?

CALVIN: More than I can count.

RAY: Ever stolen something, even if it's small, in your whole life, irrespective of its value?

CALVIN: Yes.

RAY: Ever use God's name in vain, anytime?

CALVIN: Yes.

RAY: That's using God's name in blasphemy, as a cuss word, and you've obviously looked at women with lust by the way you reacted.

CALVIN: Uh, yes.

RAY: And you've had sex before marriage?

CALVIN: Yes.

RAY: So, here's a quick summation of your Judgment Day; this is for you to judge yourself. Calvin,

you've told me you're a lying, thieving, blasphemous, fornicating adulterer at heart. So, when you
face God on Judgment Day, are you going to be
innocent or guilty?

CALVIN: Yeah, one of the two.

RAY: You'll be guilty like the rest of us.

CALVIN: Yes.

RAY: Would you therefore go to Heaven or Hell?

CALVIN: Hell.

RAY: Now, does that concern you?

CALVIN: Yes.

RAY: Man, it horrifies me. I've just met you, but I
love you. I don't want you to end up in Hell. Do you
recall the Bible verse, "The wages of sin is death"?

CALVIN: No.

RAY: It's very famous. It's saying God is paying you
in death for your sins. Like a judge looks at a criminal who thinks he's a good person, but he's committed multiple murders. The judge says, "I'm going to
show you how serious your crime is. I'm giving you
the death sentence. This is your wages, this is what
you've earned." And, Calvin, sin is so serious to a
holy God, He's given you the death sentence—
you're on Death Row. Your death will be evidence to
you that God is deadly serious about sin.

RAY [to Tyler]: Have you heard of Jesus dying on the cross for the sin of the world?

TYLER: Yes, that's another thing. How did Jesus become Son of God? How did that come out? Just out of the blue?

RAY: God was manifest in the flesh. So, let me share the gospel with you very quickly.

TYLER: You know what sounds so funny to me, hearing from you? All these questions I ask about your God, you seem to know the answers. Do you text with Him or you know Him personally? And that just blows me away—that's very arrogant to think that you know a supreme being, a guy with a beard in the sky, and you've never seen Him. You probably don't believe in aliens, huh, in spaceships? You don't believe in that? Even though there's millions of pictures of that.

RAY: Christ died for our sins. God's offering you everlasting life as a free gift if you repent and trust in Jesus. He will take the death sentence off you and…

TYLER: Surrender.

RAY: Yes, surrender. Stop the battle. You're in a place of enmity.

TYLER: It's not a battle to me!

RAY: Yes, it is.

TYLER: I don't surrender to nobody or no imaginary friend.

RAY: Okay [laughing], it's been colorful. May I give you a book I've written called *Scientific Facts in the Bible*? It'll show you the Bible is credible if you've got eyes to read it.

TYLER: No, thank you.

RAY [to Calvin]: If you can get a grip of this it's going to change everything for you, so don't let anything distract you. The Ten Commandments are called the moral Law. You and I broke the Law, Jesus paid the fine. That's what happened on that cross; that's why He said, "It is finished" just before He died. He was saying "paid in full." If you're in court and you've got speeding fines and somebody else pays them, the judge will let you go even though you're guilty. He'll say, "You're out of here. Your fine's been paid by another," and it's legal. Well, God can legally take the death sentence off you and let you live forever because Jesus paid the fine in full on that cross through His death and resurrection. And all you have to do to find everlasting life is repent of your sins, that is, turn from them, and put your trust in Jesus. Not in your goodness, but trust in Jesus, like you a trust a parachute. Calvin, if you're going to jump out of a plane at 10,000 feet, why would you put on a parachute?

CALVIN: So you can land safely.

RAY: Yes, and your motivation is fear. You fear hitting the ground at 120 miles an hour, so that fear is your friend, it's not your enemy. It's doing you a favor. It's making you put on a parachute. Calvin, because I love you, I've tried to put the fear of God in you today. I've tried to make you a little scared, hoping you'll see the seriousness of the whole situation that we're talking about, and see that fear as your friend not your enemy, because it'll make you mean business with God and put your faith in Christ where you'll find everlasting life. Is this making sense?

CALVIN: Yes, it makes sense.

RAY: Are you going to think about what we talked about?

CALVIN: Probably for the next week, yes.

RAY: I want to move away from that "probably" to a sense of urgency, because, Calvin, you don't know when you're going to die. 150,000 people die every 24 hours. And examine my tone. Why am I talking to you like this? It's because I really do care about you, and I know what I'm saying is true. I want you to think about this with a sense of urgency because this is your life we're talking about—it's not my life. I'm saved, I'm in the lifeboat. You're out there with the sharks. If death seized upon you today, you've got no recourse; you're going to be damned by God justly for your sins. So, please think about this with a sense of sobriety. Will you do that for me?

CALVIN: Yes, sir. I will.

RAY: Can I give you a book I've written called *Scientific Facts in the Bible*?

CALVIN: Sure. I can tell that you have good intentions.

RAY: I appreciate you listening to me. Let me get that book for you.

CHAPTER FOUR

IRAN HIDDEN IN PROPHECY

In Ezekiel 38:5, Scripture tells us that one of the countries that will attack Israel is Persia. Historically, Persia referred to an area located in the southwestern part of Iran. Known as the Persian Empire, it existed from approximately 550 BC to 330 BC.

In the early twentieth century, Iran was known as "Persia" in the West. The country was in a period of modernization and political change. In 1935, Reza Shah Pahlavi, the monarch of Iran, officially requested that the international community refer to the country as "Iran" instead of "Persia." This was meant to emphasize Iran's Aryan heritage and reflect the country's modern identity. "Iran" is derived from the word "Aryan," which is an ancient term referring to an ethnic group that has historical connections to the Iranian plateau.

Coincidentally, the Jew-hating Nazis also adopted the same word ("Aryan") to describe *their* ideal race:

Adolf Hitler, the leader of the Nazi Party, argued that the Germans were superior to all other races. Hitler became obsessed with "racial purity" and used the word "Aryan" to describe his idea of a "pure German race" or Herrenvolk. The "Aryan race" had a duty to control the world...

Non-Aryans came to be seen as impure and even evil. Hitler believed that Aryan superiority was being threatened particularly by the Jews. Therefore, a hierarchy of "races" was created with the Aryans at the top and with Jews, Gypsies and black people at the bottom. These "inferior" people were seen as a threat to the purity and strength of the German nation.[11]

During the Second World War, Iran became occupied by British and Soviet forces, which led to the abdication of Reza Shah in favor of his son, Mohammad Reza Shah Pahlavi, and the name remained. Officially known as the Islamic Republic of Iran since the 1979 Iranian Revolution, the country today is universally recognized as "Iran."

There are many reasons for the contention between Iran and Israel. Iran is an Islamic republic predominantly composed of Shia Muslims, while Israel is a Jewish-majority state. This religious divide has contributed to their historical enmity. Iran initially had a friendly relationship with Israel after its establishment in 1948. However, as Arab countries vehemently opposed Israel's creation, Iran was compelled to align itself with the broader Muslim world in supporting the Palestinian cause. It has done this by advocating for the rights and self-determination of Palestinians. This stance has put it in direct opposition to Israel, which it sees as the "occupier" of Palestinian lands. The enmity escalated when Iranian leaders, particularly during the presidency of Mahmoud Ahmadinejad, made statements that were highly critical of Israel. This included calls for its destruction, which further exacerbated tensions between the two nations. Iran has openly supported terrorism by backing militant groups like Hezbollah in Lebanon and Hamas in Gaza, both of which are considered enemies by Israel.

Israel has expressed serious concerns about Iran's expanding nuclear program. It fears that their pursuit of nuclear capabilities could pose a serious

threat to Israel's existence. Add to all this the fact that Iran doesn't recognize Israel as a legitimate state, leaving the two countries without diplomatic relations.

The following verses identify Iran, formerly known as Persia, as one of the countries to attack Israel:

> Thus says the Lord GOD: "Behold, I am against you, O Gog, the prince of Rosh, Meshech, and Tubal…Persia, Ethiopia, and Libya are with them, all of them with shield and helmet; Gomer and all its troops; the house of Togarmah from the far north…In the latter years you will come into the land of those brought back from the sword and gathered from many people…; they were brought out of the nations… (Ezekiel 38:3,5,6,8)

As we look back on history we can see that the Jews were "brought back from the sword and gathered from many people…; they were brought out of the nations…" Two thousand years earlier, Jesus spoke of the Jews falling by the sword and being led away into all nations:

> "And they will fall by the edge of the sword, and be led away captive into all nations. And Jerusalem will be trampled by Gentiles until the times of the Gentiles are fulfilled." (Luke 21:24)

And now "in the latter years" we see the Jew-hating nations "come into the land."

Let's look again at the passage from Ezekiel 38, where the countries that will attack Israel are actually named:

> Thus says the Lord GOD: "Behold, I am against you, O Gog, the prince of Rosh, Meshech, and Tubal…Persia, Ethiopia, and Libya are with them, all of them with shield and helmet; Gomer and all its troops; the house of Togarmah from the far north and all its troops— many people are with you." (Ezekiel 38:3,5,6)

While the names of the ancient nations may have changed over time, the locations are the same.

- Rosh: Generally seen as Russia.
- Meshech and Tubal: Often associated with regions in modern-day Turkey.
- Persia: Corresponds to present-day Iran.
- Ethiopia: Ancient Ethiopia ("Cush" in some translations) is the land south of Egypt known today as Sudan.
- Libya: The biblical region known as "Put" in some translations is modern-day Libya.
- Gomer: Part of modern Turkey.
- Togarmah: Known as ancient Armenia, this land is located within modern Turkey.

Therefore, the general consensus among most scholars is that the nations identified by name that will attack Israel in the latter years are:

Russia
Turkey
Iran
Sudan
Libya

"Many people are with you" (v. 6) may refer to other nations as well, such as Iraq, Syria, and Egypt.

We have seen how Russia has recently strengthened military ties with Iran, but is there evidence that the other named nations would have an incentive to unite in attacking Israel? You be the judge:

Turkey:

Erdogan threatens to declare war on Israel and send military to Gaza in chilling warning... The Turkish president suggested in a speech at

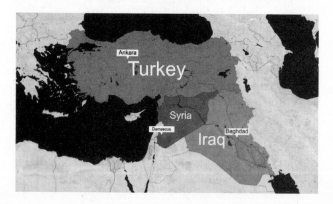

a pro-Palestine rally this afternoon that Turkey can "come at any night unexpectedly."[12]

Iran:

Iran and Israel's relationship has shifted from close cooperation, including military and economic ties, before the 1979 Iranian revolution to hostile enmity, with Iran supporting the Palestinian groups Hamas and the Islamic Jihad for Palestine again.[13]

Sudan:

Khartoum, Oct 9 (EFE) — The Sudanese Foreign Ministry announced Monday the resumption of diplomatic ties with Iran after a seven-year strain.[14]

Libya:

TRIPOLI — Libya's Tripoli-based parliament on Wednesday demanded the departure of ambassadors from countries that "support" Israel as it fights Hamas militants in Gaza, taking specific aim at the United States, Britain, France and Italy.[15]

There you have it: the countries that the Bible specified would attack the tiny nation of Israel in the latter years. And these countries are poised to do so. This isn't some nebulous prophecy pulled together by a cheap tabloid. The countries are specifically named. So we are left with the dilemma of asking whether this is a mere coincidence or whether the Scriptures are divinely inspired as they maintain they are:

> All Scripture is given by inspiration of God, and is profitable for doctrine, for reproof, for correction, for instruction in righteousness...
> (2 Timothy 3:16)

And if the Bible has proven itself to be inspired by our Creator, then its promise of everlasting life is worthy of your serious attention.

The following is a colorful conversation I had in Huntington Beach, California, with a young lady from Iran.

RAY: You are from Persia?

SARA: Yes, my ethnicity is Persian.

RAY: So, you've been following what's happening in the Middle East?

SARA: Yes.

RAY: You find it frightening?

SARA: Very so, very much so.

RAY: Do you think it could escalate into nuclear war?

SARA: That's a very good question. I think that's something we're all debating, and, you know, thinking about.

RAY: Do you ever read the Bible?

SARA: No, I'm not Christian.

RAY: Are you familiar with the Bible?

SARA: Yes.

RAY: In the Old Testament, God promised to destroy death, and in the New Testament we're told how He did it. Did you know that?

SARA: No. I don't like getting into religion.

RAY: Okay…I'll let you go. I thought you'd stay with me and see if you're a good person.

SARA: We're all good people.

RAY: Do you respect Jesus?

SARA: Yes, I do.

RAY: He said there's none good but God. Who's right, you or Him?…Question for you: are any of your friends Christians?

SARA: Yes.

RAY: They're praying for you. They care about where you'll spend eternity. That's why you're talking to me today. I knew there was something in the air, and somebody has been sharing the gospel with you. So please listen to them and think about why I'm so earnest and why I'm talking like this. It's because I know what I'm saying is true and I really do care about you. Can I give you a book I've written called *Scientific Facts in the Bible*?

SARA: Sure. Thank you. I've had these conversations for years and years and years.

RAY: Who with?

SARA: With my Christian friends, with my Jew friends, with my Muslim friends. This is never ending. You know what? At the end of the day, we all want the same thing. We all pray to the higher up. We all try our best. This is not a fair world. Just because you're Christian now, it doesn't make the world better for you or the afterlife is promised to you. If there is an afterlife.

RAY: We know there is.

SARA: No one knows what's going to happen in the next world.

RAY: Do you know eight billion people on this earth? And you know what everybody knows and what everybody doesn't know?

SARA: Nobody knows.

RAY: All you can say is *you* don't know...

SARA: Nobody knows.

RAY: The greatest authority on this earth is the Word of God. And God cannot lie. And when He says there's life after death and after death the judgment, you can rely on that. So have faith in God. Open the Bible. See what He says.

SARA: Can I tell you what my religion is?

RAY: Tell me.

SARA: There are eight billion people in this world. There are eight billion opinions in this world and eight billion beliefs in this world. And all eight billion are correct. God created all of us. And He, if He was not happy with us, He would destroy our race.

RAY: A lot of people are going to be praying for you that you come to the truth.

SARA: Thank you.

RAY: And you said about religion causing wars [Sara mentioned this earlier, off camera]. Do you know that's only 9 percent according to the *Encyclopedia of Wars*?

SARA: That's not true. Me and you are having a war right now because…

RAY: We're not!

SARA: Yes, we are. If you add hunger to it, if you add a billion other problems and poverty to it, and you're in the Middle East and we could escalate. And I'm not even defending any religion, but you're in my face. I mean, think about all the other people that come to your face. Of course, a war is going to break out. As long as people stay away from each other and don't impose their opinions, no war is going to break out.

RAY: But this is America where we have freedom of speech, and we can share our opinions without starting a war.

SARA: So, I'm saying religion always brings war.

RAY: According to the *Encyclopedia of Wars*, only 9 percent of wars are caused by religion. And most of that 9 percent are Islamic wars or the Catholic church's crusades. Christianity doesn't cause wars. We love our enemies. We do good to all men. You'll know they're Christians by their love. God is love, and I love you, and I care about you. And I'm not starting a war with you, nor an argument. I'm just here to tell you that you can have everlasting life through simply trusting in Jesus. And if you get right with God, you'll sure make your friends happy.

CHAPTER FIVE

THE COMING BATTLE

There are passages in the Bible that some believe could be a description of nuclear war, as well as its terrifying effects and devastating aftermath. These verses were written thousands of years ago in a pre-nuclear age but have extremely detailed imagery.

The first such passage is from the book of Joel. It describes something that precedes God intervening in the affairs of humanity in what is called "the great and awesome day of the Lord." Notice that what is being described leaves the reader in wonder, seems to encompass the earth to the sky, is made up of fire and pillars of smoke, and is so vast it darkens the sun and turns the moon red:

> "And I will show wonders in the heavens and in the earth: blood and fire and pillars of smoke. The sun shall be turned into darkness, and the moon into blood, before the coming of the great and awesome day of the LORD." (Joel 2:30,31)

Though "awesome" is commonly used today to refer to anything "cool," the meaning here is "terrible," "terrifying," or "dreadful." Another passage is from the book of Zechariah (written 2,600 years ago). This tells us of the frightening fate of the nations that fight against Jerusalem. God's judgment on them is something so powerful, it literally melts the human body:

> "And this shall be the plague with which the LORD will strike all the people who fought against Jerusalem:
> Their flesh shall dissolve while they stand on their feet, their eyes shall dissolve in their sockets, and their tongues shall dissolve in their mouths." (Zechariah 14:12)

Look now at these very strange instructions in the book of Ezekiel about how to bury bodies and "cleanse the land":

> "For seven months the house of Israel will be burying them, in order to cleanse the land. Indeed all the people of the land will be burying, and they will gain renown for it on the day that I am glorified," says the Lord GOD. "They will set apart men regularly employed, with the help of a search party, to pass through the land and bury those bodies remaining on the ground, in order to cleanse it. At the end of seven months they will make a search. The search party will pass through the land; and

when anyone sees a man's bone, he shall set up a marker by it, till the buriers have buried it in the Valley of Hamon Gog. The name of the city will also be Hamonah. Thus they shall cleanse the land." (Ezekiel 39:12–16)

Some suggest that the "seven months" mentioned in verse 12 could be a period of time after a catastrophic event, like a nuclear war, during which there is a prolonged process of cleaning up and burying the dead. The act of cleansing the land is perhaps dealing with the aftermath of a nuclear disaster, which would involve extensive efforts to decontaminate affected areas.

THE MYSTERY OF THE ANTICHRIST

After the 2023 attack by Hamas on Israel, and the devastating response, anyone who could bring peace between the two factions would certainly work a miracle. And so, some would say, the stage is set for that one "man of sin," the Antichrist, to bring temporary peace between the Arab and the Jew.

Let's look at the three major passages of Scripture that speak of the Antichrist, then consider those in history who fit the bill and those still living who some believe are the Antichrist:

Let no one deceive you by any means; for that Day will not come unless the falling away comes first, and the man of sin is revealed, the son of perdition, who opposes and exalts himself above all that is called God or that is worshiped, so that he sits as God in the temple of God, showing himself that he is God. (2 Thessalonians 2:3,4)

He shall speak pompous words against the Most High, shall persecute the saints of the Most High, and shall intend to change times and law. Then the saints shall be given into his hand for a time and times and half a time. (Daniel 7:25)

The coming of the lawless one is according to the working of Satan, with all power, signs, and lying wonders, and with all unrighteous deception among those who perish, because they did not receive the love of the truth, that they might be saved. (2 Thessalonians 2:9,10)

Here are a few of the historical figures who were thought by some to be the Antichrist:

In the early days of Christianity, some believed that the Roman Emperor Nero was the Antichrist due to his horrifying persecution of Christians. He certainly fit the bill.

And so did Adolf Hitler. Think of the atrocities of World War II and the Holocaust, and it's easy to see that he embodied the Antichrist.

More historic candidates have been the Pope (or the papal system). More recently, Henry Kissinger was often rumored to be the Antichrist, particularly during the Cold War era. Some also suspect Barack Obama with his leanings toward Islam. And then there are Vladimir Putin, Donald Trump, and King Charles. Some Christians are certain that Charles is the Antichrist.

I spoke about the Antichrist with two students at Cerritos College in California:

RAY: Have you heard of the Antichrist?

RUDY: Yes, I have.

RAY: Who is he?

NATALIE: Well, demon, Lucifer, and all those other things.

RAY: Do you think you could ever bring peace between the Arabs and the Jews, Israel and Hamas?

RUDY: If we're going to have world peace we've got to have some president, or something that's worth being the president, to follow.

RAY: You mean, there needs to be some figure to step up who everybody respects?

RUDY: Yes. Something like that.

RAY: You know that's something the Bible says the Antichrist will do?

RUDY: Really?

RAY: Yes. And everyone will admire him, because he's a miracle-worker who brings peace—a temporary peace that's going to explode into Armageddon. Have you heard of Armageddon?

RUDY: Yes, I have. When the Four Horsemen of the apocalypse are supposed to come, I believe?

RAY: Where'd you hear all this?

RUDY: Some of it just talking with friends who read the Bible as well.

RAY: He's a demon?

NATALIE: From what I've heard, yes. I don't really keep up with much, but when you think about Antichrist you think of demon.

RAY: Do you believe in the devil?

NATALIE: Well, yes. As a Catholic I do believe there is God and Devil.

RAY: Do you know what Satan does according to the Bible? It says the god of this world has blinded the minds of those who do not believe, lest the light of the glorious gospel of Christ—who's the image of God—should shine on them. Do you think God is justified in giving you the death sentence? Are you that evil? Or are you a good person?

NATALIE: Well, I would like to say I'm a good person. I have done a couple sins—not worthy of death.

RAY: What sort of sins?

NATALIE: Mm...like the same sex.

RAY: You mean homosexuality?

NATALIE: Yes.

RAY (to Rudy): Jesus said if you look at a woman to lust for her, you commit adultery with her in your heart. Have you ever looked at a woman with lust?

RUDY: Yes.

RAY: Sex before marriage?

RUDY: Yes.

RAY: So, Rudy, you're not a good person; you're like the rest of us. You've just told me you're a lying, thieving, blasphemous, fornicating adulterer at heart.

RUDY: Exactly. I'm a sinner. We're all sinners.

RAY: So, on Judgment Day, if God judges you by those Ten Commandments, are you going to be innocent or guilty?

NATALIE: To Him, guilty.

RAY: So, would you go to Heaven or Hell?

NATALIE: Hell.

RAY: Now does that concern you?

NATALIE: Every day.

RAY: So, this brings us to the gospel, what we were talking about in the beginning—how Satan wants to blind your mind to the glorious gospel. Let's see if he has. What did God do for guilty sinners so that we wouldn't have to go to Hell?

NATALIE: I'm unsure.

RAY: You actually know, but because Satan's blinded your mind, you don't understand it. Because you don't understand it you don't value it. Have you heard of Jesus dying on the cross?

NATALIE: Yes, I have.

RAY: Why did He do that?

NATALIE: For our sins.

RAY: What does that mean? Two thousand years later, you're in a terrible predicament of being under God's wrath. How can Jesus' death on the cross help you? How can it benefit you two thousand years later?

NATALIE: By understanding that I'm willing to die for my Savior, God.

RAY: No. Let me tell you what the Bible says.

NATALIE: Okay.

RAY: The Ten Commandments are called the moral Law. You and I broke the Law. Jesus paid the fine in full. That's why He said, "It is finished!" just before He died. He was saying, "Paid in full." If you're in court and you've got speeding fines, the judge will let you go if someone pays them. He'll say, "You're out of here, Natalie. You've got a lot of fines, but someone's paid them. You can go." God can legally dismiss your case. He can take the death sentence off you, and legally let you live forever all because of what Jesus did on the cross through His death and resurrection. And all you have to do to find everlasting life is to repent of your sin, and then trust in Jesus like you trust a parachute. So, are you going to think about what we talked about?

NATALIE: 110 percent!

RAY: There are two things you must do to be saved: You must repent of sin, and trust in Jesus. When are you going do that?

NATALIE: Starting today.

RAY: Are you serious?

NATALIE: Extremely.

RAY: Are you sorry for your sins?

NATALIE: Ten times.

RAY: Okay. Can I pray with you?

NATALIE: Of course.

RAY: Let's bow in prayer. Father, thank you for Natalie and her open heart today. I pray she'll remember her secret sins, think of Your holiness and tremble, but at the same time look at the cross and see evidence of Your great love for her. And today may her heart be broken at such incredible love, and may she truly repent and be born again and pass from death to life, all because of what Jesus did on the cross. In His name we pray, amen. Do you have a Bible at home?

NATALIE: Yes, I do.

RAY: I'm going to give you a book I wrote called *Scientific Facts in the Bible*, a little booklet called "Save Yourself Some Pain," which is principles of Christian growth, and a Gospel of John. Do you know what the Gospel of John is?

NATALIE: No.

RAY: It's the fourth book of the New Testament.

RAY [to Rudy]: Is this making sense?

RUDY: Yes, sir, it does.

RAY: Are you going to think about what we talked about?

RUDY: Yes, it's going to be on my mind all day today.

RAY: So, when are you going to repent and put your faith in Christ?

RUDY: Um, today?

RAY: You realize you're giving up the battle? You're saying, "God, You gave me life. I give it back to You." Are you sorry for your sins?

RUDY: I am. I am sorry for my sins.

RAY: Can I pray with you?

RUDY: Sure.

RAY: Let's bow in prayer. Father, I pray for Rudy. Thank You for his open heart today and his willingness to acknowledge his sins. I pray You'll grant him repentance and that You'll bring him out of darkness into light and he'll understand the gravity of his sin and the love You've expressed through that cross. May today he be born again and have a new heart and new desires and love righteousness and love You, all because of Your amazing grace. In Jesus' name we pray, amen.

• • •

So we are left asking, "Who is the Antichrist?" Is it a pseudo-Christian system that has persecuted genuine Christians throughout the ages, one evil historical figure, or will it be a man in the future who will bring temporary peace in the Middle East—only to usher in Armageddon? Time will tell.

In the meanwhile, we live in an extremely volatile world—one that is wracked by great earthquakes, terrible famines, and deadly pestilences. It is a world where nation is rising against nation and kingdom against kingdom, where there are wars and rumors of wars, where lawlessness abounds, where Islamic nations are bearing down on Israel, and where men's hearts are failing them from fear of that which is coming on the earth.

The Jews have Jerusalem, and that tiny city has become a burdensome stone for all the nations—as prophesied by Zechariah more than 2,500 years ago:

> Behold, I will make Jerusalem a cup of trembling unto all the people round about, when they shall be in the siege both against Judah and against Jerusalem. And in that day will I make Jerusalem a burdensome stone for all people: all that burden themselves with it shall be cut in pieces, though all the people of the earth be gathered together against it. (Zechariah 12:2,3, KJV)

Just after Jesus said that Jerusalem would be given back into Jewish hands—which happened in 1967—He said these words:

> "Now when these things begin to happen, look up and lift up your heads, because your redemption draws near." (Luke 21:28)

When we see these frightening things happening, we are to look up in expectation, not look down in fear of the future. We're not waiting for the end of the world but for a world without end—the beginning of a new one—where God's kingdom will come to this earth and His will will be done on earth as it is in Heaven:

> The word that Isaiah the son of Amoz saw concerning Judah and Jerusalem.
>
> Now it shall come to pass in the latter days
> That the mountain of the LORD's house
> Shall be established on the top of the moun-
>   tains,
> And shall be exalted above the hills;
> And all nations shall flow to it.
> Many people shall come and say,
> "Come, and let us go up to the mountain of
>   the LORD,
> To the house of the God of Jacob;
> He will teach us His ways,
> And we shall walk in His paths."
> For out of Zion shall go forth the law,
> And the word of the LORD from Jerusalem.
> He shall judge between the nations,
> And rebuke many people;
> They shall beat their swords into plowshares,
> And their spears into pruning hooks;
> Nation shall not lift up sword against nation,
> Neither shall they learn war anymore.
> (Isaiah 2:1–4)

My wife, Sue, and I are big fans of the sport of rugby. But when our favorite team is playing we can't watch it live. It is too stressful. And so we only watch replays, *and we only do that when we know*

that our team won. That doesn't ruin the game for
us, because there's a wonderful silver lining. We
never get even slightly stressed *since we know that we
win in the end.* When the opposing team roars as
they score, we just smile, because we know what's
coming.

That's why we should never become fearful, no
matter how great the opposition—*because we know
what happens in the end.* Righteousness will prevail.
God will have His perfect will. You can be sure of
that.

And while we wait for that day, here are twenty
wonderful promises from the Word of God that will
help you guard your heart and mind from any fear
of the future:

1. "Fear not, for I am with you; be not dismayed,
   for I am your God. I will strengthen you, yes, I
   will help you, I will uphold you with My righteous right hand." (Isaiah 41:10)

2. "I sought the LORD, and He heard me, and
   delivered me from all my fears." (Psalm 34:4)

3. "Have I not commanded you? Be strong and of
   good courage; do not be afraid, nor be dismayed,
   for the LORD your God is with you wherever
   you go." (Joshua 1:9)

4. "And the LORD, He is the One who goes before
   you. He will be with you, He will not leave you

nor forsake you; do not fear nor be dismayed."
(Deuteronomy 31:8)

5. "Yea, though I walk through the valley of the
   shadow of death, I will fear no evil; for You are
   with me; Your rod and Your staff, they comfort
   me." (Psalm 23:4)

6. "And David said to his son Solomon, 'Be strong
   and of good courage, and do it; do not fear nor
   be dismayed, for the LORD God—my God—will
   be with you. He will not leave you nor forsake
   you, until you have finished all the work for the
   service of the house of the LORD.'" (1 Chron-
   icles 28:20)

7. "But now, thus says the LORD, who created you,
   O Jacob, and He who formed you, O Israel:
   'Fear not, for I have redeemed you; I have called
   you by your name; You are Mine. When you
   pass through the waters, I will be with you; and
   through the rivers, they shall not overflow you.
   When you walk through the fire, you shall not
   be burned, nor shall the flame scorch you.'"
   (Isaiah 43:1,2)

8. "The LORD is my light and my salvation; whom
   shall I fear? The LORD is the strength of my life;
   of whom shall I be afraid?" (Psalm 27:1)

9. "For I am persuaded that neither death nor life,
   nor angels nor principalities nor powers, nor

things present nor things to come, nor height nor depth, nor any other created thing, shall be able to separate us from the love of God which is in Christ Jesus our Lord." (Romans 8:38,39)

10. "Whenever I am afraid, I will trust in You. In God (I will praise His word), in God I have put my trust; I will not fear. What can flesh do to me?" (Psalm 56:3,4)

11. "Trust in the LORD with all your heart, and lean not on your own understanding; in all your ways acknowledge Him, and He shall direct your paths." (Proverbs 3:5,6)

12. "Therefore do not worry about tomorrow, for tomorrow will worry about its own things. Sufficient for the day is its own trouble." (Matthew 6:34)

13. "Peace I leave with you, My peace I give to you; not as the world gives do I give to you. Let not your heart be troubled, neither let it be afraid." (John 14:27)

14. "For God has not given us a spirit of fear, but of power and of love and of a sound mind." (2 Timothy 1:7)

15. "He shall cover you with His feathers, and under His wings you shall take refuge; His truth shall be your shield and buckler." (Psalm 91:4)

16. "The LORD is on my side; I will not fear. What can man do to me?" (Psalm 118:6)

17. "Let your conduct be without covetousness; be content with such things as you have. For He Himself has said, 'I will never leave you nor forsake you.' So we may boldly say: 'The LORD is my helper; I will not fear. What can man do to me?'" (Hebrews 13:5,6)

18. "Be anxious for nothing, but in everything by prayer and supplication, with thanksgiving, let your requests be made known to God; and the peace of God, which surpasses all understanding, will guard your hearts and minds through Christ Jesus." (Philippians 4:6,7)

19. "The LORD your God in your midst, the Mighty One, will save; He will rejoice over you with gladness, He will quiet you with His love, He will rejoice over you with singing." (Zephaniah 3:17)

20. "And when I saw Him, I fell at His feet as dead. But He laid His right hand on me, saying to me, 'Do not be afraid; I am the First and the Last.'" (Revelation 1:17)

And whatever the future brings our way, never forget this dying world and our moral obligation to reach out to them. Our hearts should break at the thought of anyone facing death without faith in the Savior. Listen to the words of Jesus:

> "And this gospel of the kingdom will be preached in all the world as a witness to all the nations, and then the end will come." (Matthew 24:14)

• • •

Help us to get the gospel to all the world by passing this book on to others. You can find details on how to get the book at very low-cost bulk pricing or as a free digital version at LivingWaters.com. It is also available without charge in Hebrew and Arabic (and other languages) at LivingWaters.com/volatile.

NOTES

1. "Is Vladimir Putin the Prophesied 'Prince of Rosh'?" *The Philadelphia Trumpet*, February 2014 <thetrumpet.com/11228-is-vladimir-putin-the-prophesied-prince-of-rosh>.

2. "Lockyer's *All the Men of the Bible*—Rosh" <biblegateway.com/resources/all-men-bible/Rosh>.

3. *McClintock and Strong Biblical Cyclopedia* <biblical cyclopedia.com/R/rosh.html>.

4. "Does the Bible say anything about Russia in relation to the end times?" <gotquestions.org/Russia-end-times.html>.

5. Mary Miller, "The Treacherous Trio of Ezekiel 38 Part 3: Russia," Koinonia Institute, August 1, 2009 <khouse.org/articles/2009/869>.

6. "2022 Report on International Religious Freedom: Russia," Office of International Religious Freedom <tinyurl.com/religious-freedom-russia>.

7. "Iran & Russia: Burgeoning Military Ties," United States Institute of Peace, September 5, 2023 <iranprimer.usip.org/blog/2023/may/18/iran-russia-burgeoning-military-ties>.

8. Interview with chemistry professor: "Try and Keep Up With His Brain. Bet You Can't" <youtube.com/watch?v=0Dl1XlK0VUw>.

9. Wayne Jackson, "Was the Gospel Preached throughout the 'Whole World' in the First Century?" Christian Courier <christiancourier.com/articles/was-the-gospel-preached-throughout-the-whole-world-in-the-first-century>.

10. "What does it mean that a prophecy has a double/dual fulfillment?" GotQuestions <gotquestions.org/prophecy-double-dual-fulfillment.html>. Published with permission.

11. "How did the Nazis construct an Aryan identity?" South African History Online <sahistory.org.za/article/how-did-nazis-construct-aryan-identity>.

12. "Erdogan threatens to declare war on Israel and send military to Gaza in chilling warning," *Express*, October 28, 2023 <express.co.uk/news/world/1829092/Erdogan-Turkey-Israel-war-Gaza>.

13. "From friends to foes: How Iranian-Israeli relations transformed over 70 years," *The New Arab*, October 23, 2023 <newarab.com/news/how-iran-and-israel-went-being-allies-bitter-foes>.

14. "Sudan, Iran decide to restore diplomatic ties amid Israel-Palestine war," October 9, 2023 <efe.com/en/other-news/2023-10-09/sudan-iran-decide-to-restore-diplomatic-ties-amid-israel-palestine-war>.

15. "Libya Parliament Orders Out Diplomats of Countries Supporting Israel," October 25, 2023 <voaafrica.com/a/libya-parliament-orders-out-diplomats-from-countries-supporting-israel-/7326552.html>.